The 21st Century 80-20 learner and Learnings Approach

Ultimate Guide To Hone Your Skills Improve Learning Speed and Learn How To Memorize Anything

Dr. David M. Hills

Disclaimer

This publication is designed to provide accurate, reliable and authoritative information in regards to the subject matter covered. The author and publisher do not assume any responsibility for errors, inaccuracies or omissions.

By it's sale, neither the publisher not the author is engaged in rendering or other professional services. If expert assistance, and guidance is needed, the services of a competent and skillful professional should be sought.

Writer Bio

Meet Dr. David M. Hills, the knowledge architect and creative force behind "The 21st Century 80-20 Learner and Learning Approach." David is a polymath when it comes to learning and personal growth. He infuses every page of this revolutionary manual with enthusiasm, a depth of experience, and a dedication to perfection.

David M. Hills is a seasoned traveler of the wide landscapes of knowledge, not just a writer. Using his varied experience in technology, teaching, and entrepreneurship, David has developed into a real 80-20 learner. His unquenchable curiosity and unwavering drive for efficiency have made him a forerunner in the field of contemporary learning approaches.

David has devoted his professional life to comprehending the nuances of skill mastery, quick learning, and the smooth integration of technology into education as an advocate for continual development. His path has led him through the halls of conventional higher education, the frontiers of digital innovation, and the life-changing terrain of personal development.

Beyond his accomplishments in the business world, David M. Hills has always had a passion for learning. His love of learning transcends the pages of this book to the communities he interacts with and the mentoring he offers to individuals who want to discover their limitless capacity for learning.

David's distinct viewpoint, driven by a growth mentality and an uncompromising dedication to quality, establishes the foundation for "The 21st Century 80-20 Learner and Learning Approach." He extends an invitation to readers to go with him through this book, where pursuing knowledge is not only a decision but a way of life, and where opportunities are endless, limited only by one's curiosity and commitment.

Examine the world of education through David M. Hills's perspective, and allow his ideas, methods, and enthusiasm for lifelong learning to motivate you to take charge of your intellectual development. You're not just reading a book when you go on an adventure with David as your guide; you're going on a journey that takes you beyond the ordinary and toward the remarkable.

Book Description

Embark on a revolutionary journey into the core of modern learning with "The 21st Century 80-20 Learner and Learning Approach." This engaging guide is your key to discovering the principles of efficient learning, rapid skill mastery, and the art of memorization in the digital age.

Discover the ideas of the 80-20 learner and somebody committed to attaining maximum results with the least effort. From unleashing the 80-20 learning revolution to turbocharging your learning speed and unlocking your memory potential through the art of mnemonics, each chapter is a treasure mine of tactics designed to make your learning experience not only successful but exhilarating.

But this book is more than simply a guidebook; it's an invitation to become an infinite learner a seeker of information, a master of skills, and a lifelong enthusiast in the quest for perfection. Dive into the world of technology and learn how to harness it for optimal learning results, from online platforms and educational apps to virtual reality and adaptive learning systems.

The trip doesn't end there. Cultivate a lifelong learning mindset that transcends traditional boundaries, accepts obstacles, and views learning not as a destination but as an unlimited horizon. This is not just a book; it's a passport to boundless discovery, an expedition where the pages are doorways to other worlds, and each chapter is a stepping stone toward unlocking the infinite learner within you.

Whether you're a student, a professional, or an individual hungry for personal improvement, this book is your guide to becoming an architect of your intellectual destiny. The adventure begins now immerse yourself in the art, science, and philosophy of learning, and let the transformative journey unfold. Join the ranks of the 80-20 learners who dance on the edge of what's possible, driven by a passion for understanding and a dedication to improvement.

Are you ready to sharpen your abilities, accelerate your learning, and explore the endless opportunities that await the 21st-century learner? If so, this book is your ticket to a world where knowledge has no limitations, and the voyage of learning is as fascinating as the places it unveils. Buy your copy now and journey into a future defined by the ravenous quest for knowledge and the boundless possibilities that unfurl with each discovery.

Introduction

Unleashing the Infinite Learner

In the great expanse of the 21st century, when information is the currency of progress, the need to become an endless learner echoes louder than ever before. As we traverse a world sculpted by fast breakthroughs, unforeseen obstacles, and extraordinary opportunities, the ability to learn continually emerges not just as a skill but as a transformative mindset the key to unlocking untapped potential and charting a road toward mastery.

Picture a journey where curiosity is the compass, adaptation is the vessel, and growth is the destination. This is the adventure we go upon, motivated by the principles of the 80-20 learner a seeker of efficiency, a master of skill, and a lifelong devotee in the quest for knowledge. In the pages that follow, we investigate the difficult tapestry of learning in the digital era, weaving together methodologies, insights, and practical guidance to support you on your journey to becoming an eternal learner.

From the art of efficient learning and the secrets of rapid skill acquisition to the melding of technology and timeless wisdom, each chapter offers a gateway to a new realm of possibilities. Here, you'll discover how to navigate the immense expanses of knowledge, leveraging the resources of the digital world to accelerate your learning to new heights. But beyond the practicalities, this voyage is also a fundamental exploration of attitude a mindset that transcends traditional bounds, accepts challenges as possibilities, and regards learning not as a goal but as a limitless horizon.

As we delve into the chapters that follow, imagine yourself not only as a reader but as an adventurer, a seeker of wisdom, and an architect of your intellectual future. The 80-20 learner is not restricted by limits; rather, they dance on the edges of what's possible, inspired by a love for understanding, a dedication to growth, and a tireless pursuit of greatness.

Welcome to a tour where the books are doorways to other planets, and each chapter is a stepping stone toward unleashing the boundless learner within you. The adventure begins now immerse yourself in the art, science, and philosophy of learning, and let the transformative journey unfold. Together, let's start on a quest to free the endless learner the builder of a future defined by the unquenchable hunger for knowledge and the unlimited possibilities that emerge with each discovery.

Chapter 1

Unleashing the 80-20 Learning Revolution

In the broad terrain of education and human development, a revolution is silently taking place an evolution of learning that surpasses established paradigms. Welcome to the 80-20 Learning Revolution, where the force of the Pareto Principle transforms the way we gain knowledge and skills in the 21st century.

The Hidden Key to Unlocking Potential

The adventure begins with an exploration of the Pareto Principle, frequently referred to as the 80-20 rule. Italian economist Vilfredo Pareto initially noted that around 80% of effects come from 20% of causes. Little did he anticipate that this theory would become a cornerstone in understanding how we learn and, more crucially, how we may learn more efficiently.

Consider the implications: What if we could focus on the crucial 20% of information that adds to 80% of our understanding? What if we could pinpoint the main variables that drive skill development and enhance our learning speed? The 80-20 Learning Revolution answers these concerns and more, promising a paradigm shift in the way we approach education.

Breaking Free from Information Overload

In an era defined by information overload, the 80-20 Learning Revolution offers a lifeline to people drowning in a sea of data. The traditional approach to learning frequently entails a linear, comprehensive search for knowledge. However, the 80-20 learner embraces a non-linear technique, isolating the most vital components of a subject and focusing on them with laser-like accuracy.

Imagine a world where you could learn more in less time, where the quality of knowledge outweighs the quantity. The 80-20 Learning Revolution is not simply a tactic; it's an attitude that empowers learners to break free from the shackles of information saturation.

The Anatomy of the 80-20 Learner

What distinguishes the 80-20 learner from the ordinary learner? It's a mindset that prioritizes efficiency, effectiveness, and mastery. This chapter digs into the characteristics of the 80-20 learner, addressing skills such as discernment, strategic focus, and a dedication to ongoing growth.

We'll study real-world instances of individuals who have adopted the 80-20 approach, completing incredible things in record time. From polymaths who master numerous topics to professionals who rapidly advance the ranks of their industries, the 80-20 learner is not restricted by conventional bounds.

The Power of Selective Learning

At the heart of the 80-20 Learning Revolution is the art of selective learning. This section helps readers through the process of determining the crucial 20% of information that generates 80% of the results. Whether you're studying for an exam, mastering a new skill, or digging into a complex subject, the ability to differentiate the crucial from the trivial is a skill that sets the 80-20 learner distinct.

Through actionable ideas, informative examples, and hands-on exercises, readers will learn to utilize selective learning in their educational pursuits. The idea is not merely to ingest information but to digest it with purpose and intention.

Embarking on Your 80-20 Learning Journey

As we complete this chapter, readers are invited to go on their own 80-20 learning journey. The revolution begins with a shift in perspective, a willingness to question the existing quo, and a commitment to embracing a more effective and efficient approach to learning.

The 80-20 Learning Revolution is not a one-size-fits-all solution; rather, it's a flexible framework that adjusts to individual goals and learning styles. In the chapters that follow, we will delve deeper into the tactics, techniques, and attitudes that define the 80-20 learner, empowering you to unleash your full learning potential in the 21st century. Get ready to alter your approach to education and start on a transforming path toward mastery and expertise. The 80-20 Learning Revolution awaits.

Chapter 2

Strategies for Turbocharging Your Learning Speed

In the fascinating adventure of learning, time is often of the essence. The ability to absorb, process, and retain knowledge swiftly is a hallmark of the 80-20 learner. In this chapter, we'll delve into the dynamic world of techniques aimed to turbocharge your learning speed, arming you with the tools to become a speedy and effective knowledge assimilator.

The Need for Speed in Learning

Before we investigate the solutions, let's dissect why speed matters in the context of learning. In a fast-paced world where information is continually developing, the ability to keep pace is a competitive advantage. Whether you're a student aiming for academic achievement, a professional looking to stay ahead in your business, or an enthusiast willing to study varied subjects, learning rapidly is a skill that opens doors to new opportunities.

Speed Reading: Beyond the Words

At the forefront of learning speed is the art of fast reading. It's not just about reading swiftly but also about boosting understanding. We'll explore the basics of rapid reading, guiding readers through tactics such as chunking, limiting subvocalization, and employing peripheral vision. Through practical activities, you'll observe a revolution in your reading speed without losing your understanding.

Active Learning: Engaging the Mind

The 80-20 learner knows that passive absorption of knowledge is inefficient. Active learning entails engaging with the subject actively, encouraging deeper knowledge and retention. We'll study approaches such as summarizing, teaching the content to others, and applying knowledge through real-world settings. By becoming an active participant in the learning process, you'll improve your comprehension and learning speed concurrently.

Optimizing Cognitive Processes

The human brain is a powerful instrument, and enhancing its cognitive processes can dramatically boost learning speed. We'll go into the science of neuroplasticity, addressing techniques to boost memory, focus, and information processing. From including brain-boosting items into your diet to adopting mindfulness techniques, these strategies will ensure that your cognitive engine functions at full performance.

Multisensory Learning: Engaging All Facets

Learning is not only a visual experience. The 80-20 learner realizes the necessity of activating several senses to boost learning speed. This section addresses the benefits of multimodal learning, combining auditory, kinesthetic, and tactile elements into your study regimen. By tapping into different sensory pathways, you'll create a deeper and more memorable learning experience.

Strategic Note-Taking: Capture and Condense

Effective note-taking is an often-overlooked factor of learning speed. We'll reveal the art of smart note-taking, teaching you how to collect key information efficiently and condense it for easy review. Whether you like digital note-taking tools or the old pen-and-paper method, you'll discover a system that corresponds with your learning style.

Harnessing Technology for Accelerated Learning

In the digital age, technology may be a tremendous ally in turbocharging your learning speed. We'll explore innovative tools and apps meant to enhance the learning experience. From AI-driven study aids to interactive learning platforms, you'll get insights on harnessing technology for better learning results.

Continuous Improvement: Iterative Learning Speed

The journey to turbocharge your learning speed is a continuous process of refining. We'll cover the importance of feedback loops, self-assessment, and iterative improvements. By embracing a mindset of continual learning and adaptability, you'll consistently boost your learning speed over time.

As we end this chapter, you'll not only have a toolset of tactics at your disposal but also a stronger grasp of the principles that govern rapid learning. Whether you're hoping to tackle large volumes of material or seeking to acquire a new talent rapidly, the tactics outlined in this chapter will accelerate you toward becoming a strong 80-20 learner. Get ready to unleash the full potential of your learning speed and go on a journey of faster information acquisition.

Chapter 3

The Art of Mnemonics: Unlocking Your Memory Potential

In the maze of learning, memory stands as a strong gatekeeper. The ability to retain knowledge quickly and accurately is a superpower held by the excellent learner. In this chapter, we'll delve into the beautiful realm of mnemonics a timeless technique that acts as the key to unlocking your memory potential and transforming you into a masterful 80-20 learner.

The Memory Maze: Understanding Memory Function

Before we continue on our examination of mnemonics, it's necessary to solve the mysteries of memory. We'll voyage across the realms of short-term and long-term memory, investigating the cognitive processes that govern the encoding, storage, and retrieval of information. Understanding the nuances of memory will offer the foundation for harnessing its full potential through the artful use of mnemonics.

Mnemonics Unveiled: The Memory Aide

Mnemonics, derived from the ancient Greek word "mnēmōn," meaning "mindful," are memory enhancers that assist in information retention. We'll examine the numerous sorts of mnemonics, from acronyms and acrostics to rhymes and associations. Each mnemonic device has its distinct appeal, offering a creative and effective technique to stamp knowledge on the canvas of your memory.

Creating Mnemonic Masterpieces

Crafting mnemonic devices is an art that converts the banal into the memorable. This section will walk you through the process of making your mnemonic masterpieces. Whether you're memorizing a list of things, a sequence of numbers, or complicated concepts, you'll learn to adjust your mnemonics to suit the nature of the information you wish to recall.

The Memory Palace: Architectural Mnemonics

Among the pantheon of mnemonic techniques, the Memory Palace ranks as a crowning treasure. Originating from ancient Rome, this strategy includes mentally putting information within the rooms of an imaginary palace. We'll study the nuances of developing your

Memory Palace, unlocking the possibility of memorizing massive amounts of knowledge in a structured and remembered fashion.

Association Magic: Linking the Unrelated

At the heart of mnemonics lies the power of association. This section dives into the technique of linking seemingly unrelated things through vivid and imaginative analogies. By constructing mental connections and narratives, you'll discover how to forge enduring relationships between pieces of information, ensuring their retrieval becomes a smooth and intuitive process.

Advanced Mnemonics for Complex Learning

As we go, we'll disclose sophisticated mnemonics for tackling hard subjects and detailed knowledge. From the Major System for memorizing numbers to the Journey Method for sequential knowledge, you'll add flexible tools to your mnemonic arsenal. These skills will equip you to tackle the most complicated issues with confidence and finesse.

Memory Maintenance: The Mnemonic Routine

Building a powerful memory entails not just creating mnemonics but also sustaining and reinforcing them. This section covers ways for regular mnemonic review, ensuring that the information stays fresh and easily retrievable throughout time. From spaced repetition techniques to adding mnemonic rituals into your daily routine, you'll create a memory that's sharp, trustworthy, and available when you need it.

Real-World Applications: Mnemonics in Action

To strengthen your understanding, we'll study real-world uses of mnemonics. Whether you're a student studying for examinations, a professional recalling crucial material for presentations, or a person looking to remember names and faces effortlessly, mnemonics offer a comprehensive set of tools that transcend academic borders.

Embarking on Your Mnemonic Odyssey

As we complete this chapter, you stand at the brink of a mnemonic odyssey an investigation of your memory potential. Armed with an array of mnemonic strategies and a solid understanding of memory function, you're set to unleash the full possibilities of your mind. Mnemonics isn't simply an art; it's a dynamic skill that affects the way you see and retain information. Get ready to embark on a trip where the nuances of your memory become a canvas for mnemonic mastery. The art of mnemonics awaits, ready to unlock the unlimited potential of your memory and catapult you to the ranks of the genuinely skilled learner.

Chapter 4

Hone Your Skills: A Blueprint for Mastery

Mastery is not a destination but a journey one that the 80-20 learner approaches with strategic intent. In this chapter, we embark on a revolutionary investigation of skill development, exposing a complete plan meant to assist you on the path to mastery.

The Mastery Mindset: Crafting Your Skill Development Philosophy

Before we go into the blueprint, it's necessary to build the correct mentality for skill development. This section covers the characteristics of the mastery mindset, emphasizing the need for patience, perseverance, and a real passion for the chosen talent. Understanding the attitude that underlies skill acquisition creates the framework for a meaningful and rewarding path.

Identifying Your Skill Set: Navigating Your Talents and Passions

The first step in the blueprint entails a deep dive into self-discovery. We'll study ways to identify your existing abilities, natural talents, and areas of enthusiasm. By linking your skill development with your intrinsic interests, you'll establish a sense of purpose that propels you ahead on the path to mastery.

Setting SMART Goals: The North Star of Skill Development

Goals are the compass that guides your skill development journey. We'll introduce the SMART criteria Specific, Measurable, Achievable, Relevant, and Time-bound to help you establish clear and concrete goals. Whether you're looking to learn a musical instrument, master a computer language, or increase a professional skill, setting SMART goals offers a disciplined and achievable approach.

Deliberate Practice: The Engine of Skill Mastery

Deliberate practice is the secret sauce underlying skill mastery. This section dissects the components of intentional practice, highlighting the need for concentrated, systematic, and repeating activities. From breaking down complex talents into digestible components to seeking feedback for continuous development, intentional practice becomes the engine that propels you toward mastery.

Feedback Loop: The Catalyst for Improvement

Constructive feedback is a critical factor in the skill development path. We'll study how to construct a feedback loop, requesting information from mentors, peers, or simply self-assessment. By studying and applying feedback, you'll develop your approach, correct mistakes, and continuously elevate your skill level.

Embracing Discomfort: The Growth Zone

Skill improvement typically means moving outside your comfort zone. We'll address the concept of the growth zone, where challenges and discomfort become catalysts for learning. By embracing rather than avoiding suffering, you'll access new levels of skill learning and personal growth.

Interdisciplinary Learning: Broadening Your Skill Horizon

The 80-20 learner appreciates the significance of transdisciplinary learning. This section covers how obtaining talents from other domains can enrich your primary skill set. Whether through the integration of complementing talents or the application of principles from other areas, interdisciplinary learning offers possibilities for creative problem-solving and creativity.

Building a Skill Arsenal: Layering and Combining Skills

Skill mastery is often a composite of individual proficiencies. We'll learn how to layer and mix talents to create a unique and powerful skill arsenal. Whether in the fields of creativity, technology, or leadership, the ability to synthesize multiple skills lays the foundation for unprecedented mastery.

Creating a Learning Routine: Consistency in Skill Development

Consistency is the key to skill improvement. We'll aid you in developing a learning schedule that corresponds with your lifestyle and goals. From time management tactics to building a dedicated learning environment, a well-crafted routine ensures that skill development becomes an intrinsic part of your everyday life.

The Mastery Portfolio: Showcasing Your Progress

A mastery portfolio becomes a witness to your skill development journey. We'll study how to construct a visual depiction of your progress, documenting achievements, projects, and milestones. The mastery portfolio serves not only as a personal record but also as a great tool for showing your abilities to potential employers, clients, or colleagues.

Navigating Plateaus: Overcoming Skill Development Challenges

The skill development journey is not without its hurdles. Plateaus, periods of stagnation, are a typical occurrence. We'll cover tactics for navigating and conquering plateaus, ensuring that failures become stepping stones toward greater expertise.

Celebrating Milestones: Acknowledging Progress

Amidst the journey toward mastery, it's vital to celebrate milestones. We'll explore the significance of appreciating successes, both great and small. Celebrations not only encourage but also build a good outlook, moving you onward with renewed excitement.

Giving Back: The Mastery Community

The final component of the blueprint involves giving back to the mastering community. Whether through mentorship, knowledge-sharing, or collaborative projects, contributing to the community strengthens your expertise while building a culture of shared learning.

As we complete this chapter, you now hold a blueprint for skill mastery a roadmap that integrates mindset, goal-setting, focused practice, and continual development. Armed with this blueprint, you're prepared to go on a revolutionary path toward mastering the abilities that mean most to you. Get ready to develop your abilities, uncover your potential, and become a real 80-20 learner on the path to mastery. The voyage awaits, and the blueprint is your route to competent perfection.

Chapter 5

Leveraging Technology for Optimal Learning

In the dynamic terrain of 21st-century learning, technology stands as a formidable ally, offering a plethora of tools and resources to enhance the learning experience. This chapter offers a deep dive into the strategic integration of technology, providing a detailed guide on how to harness digital resources for optimal learning results. From online platforms to cutting-edge applications, this chapter highlights the wide technology environment meant to assist you on your 80-20 learning journey.

Understanding the Digital Learning Landscape: Navigating the Ecosystem

The digital learning landscape is vast, spanning a myriad of platforms, applications, and resources. In this section, we'll begin on a tour around the digital ecosystem, investigating the numerous components that contribute to an enriched learning experience. From online classes and instructional apps to collaborative tools, comprehending the digital environment is the first step toward employing technology effectively.

Online Learning Platforms: Beyond Traditional Classrooms

Online learning systems have changed education, giving flexibility and accessibility. We'll look into prominent platforms such as Coursera, edX, and Khan Academy, evaluating their distinct features, course offerings, and learning methods. Discover how these platforms can be leveraged to enhance traditional learning or serve as standalone tools for skill development.

Educational Apps: Mobile Learning at Your Fingertips

Mobile technology has ushered in an era of on-the-go learning. This section discusses educational apps that appeal to a spectrum of subjects and skills. From language learning applications like Duolingo to coding platforms such as Codecademy, you'll unearth a treasure trove of apps designed to make learning entertaining, interactive, and suited to your speed and tastes.

Digital Libraries and Open Educational Resources: Knowledge Without Borders

Digital libraries and free educational resources tear down barriers to information access. We'll explore platforms like Project Gutenberg, Google Scholar, and OpenStax, giving a variety of textbooks, academic papers, and literary classics. Learn how to navigate these resources effectively, broadening your knowledge base without the limits of traditional libraries.

Virtual Reality (VR) and Augmented Reality (AR): Immersive Learning Experiences

Immersive technologies like VR and AR are altering the learning landscape. This section introduces you to programs that enable virtual field trips, 3D simulations, and augmented reality overlays for hands-on experiences. Explore how these technologies bring subjects to life, making complex concepts tangible and increasing your understanding in unforeseen ways.

Adaptive Learning Systems: Tailoring Education to Your Needs

Adaptive learning systems leverage artificial intelligence to tailor educational experiences based on individual achievement and preferences. We'll look into platforms like Smart Sparrow and DreamBox, explaining how adaptive systems give tailored learning routes, real-time feedback, and targeted interventions to maximize your learning journey.

Collaboration Tools: Learning in Community

Learning is a social undertaking, and collaboration technologies enable engagement and information sharing. Explore services like Slack, Microsoft Teams, and Google Workspace, which offer collaborative tasks, group conversations, and seamless communication. Discover how these tools transform lonely studying into a collaborative and engaging experience.

Gamification and Learning: Turning Education into Play

Gamification injects elements of game design into educational activities, making learning more engaging and pleasant. This section covers platforms like Kahoot! and Quizizz, where quizzes become games, and achievements unlock additional levels of knowledge. Uncover the psychology of gamification and how it promotes motivation and retention.

Digital Note-Taking and Organization: Streamlining Your Learning Process

Efficient note-taking and organizing are key parts of optimal learning. We'll investigate digital applications like Evernote, OneNote, and Notion, which offer capabilities such as cross-device syncing, multimedia integration, and collaborative editing. Learn how these tools streamline the gathering and management of information, turning your digital workspace into a hive of productivity.

Blockchain in Education: Verifying Credentials and Continuous Learning

Blockchain technology is redefining credential verification and continuous learning. Discover platforms like Learning Machine and BitDegree that use blockchain to safeguard and confirm educational credentials. Understand how this technology is altering the certification market, enabling a transparent and decentralized approach to recognizing talents and achievements.

Ethical Considerations in Educational Technology: Navigating Challenges

As we embrace the promise of instructional technology, ethical questions come to the forefront. This section addresses problems such as data privacy, digital divide issues, and the possible perils of algorithmic prejudice. Gain insights into navigating the ethical world of educational technology, ensuring that your digital learning path corresponds with ideals of fairness and diversity.

Strategies for Effective Digital Learning Integration: A Holistic Approach

Integrating technology into your learning journey demands a smart strategy. We'll present full guidance on building a digital learning strategy, including goal formulation, resource selection, and time management. Discover how to find a balance between traditional and digital learning methods, developing a holistic strategy that leverages the benefits of both.

Continuous Learning in the Digital Age: Embracing Lifelong Education

The digital world promotes constant learning, and this part investigates ways to build a mindset of perpetual education. From microlearning platforms to social media communities, find channels that encourage continuing skill development and keep you updated on the current developments in your chosen industry.

As we end this chapter, you'll emerge equipped with the knowledge to harness technology for the best learning. The digital universe is enormous, but with careful navigation, you may harness these technologies to amplify your 80-20 learning trip. Embrace the possibilities, experiment with multiple platforms, and uncover the full power of technology as your learning friend in the 21st century. The digital environment is yours to explore, and the tools within it are ready to empower you in your quest for knowledge and skill development.

Chapter 6

Cultivating A Lifelong Learning Mindset

In the ever-evolving world of the 21st century, the ability to learn continuously is not simply a valued skill; it's a mindset that propels individuals toward personal and professional success. This chapter offers a deep study into creating a lifelong learning mindset a dynamic approach that welcomes curiosity, adaptation, and unrelenting dedication to improvement. Join us on a transformative journey as we unravel the concepts, tactics, and habits that underpin a mentality of lifelong learning.

Understanding Lifelong Learning: A Mindset for the Modern World

Lifelong learning extends conventional education, embracing a dedication to obtaining knowledge and skills over one's entire life. In this section, we'll lay the basis by defining lifelong learning and explaining its value in a society where flexibility and ongoing growth are key.

The Growth Mindset: Embracing Challenges and Learning from Failure

Central to the lifelong learning mindset is the concept of the growth mindset. We'll investigate the pioneering work of psychologist Carol Dweck, who proposed the idea that intelligence and abilities can be enhanced through devotion and hard effort. Learn how to create a growth mentality that accepts difficulties, perseveres in the face of setbacks, and sees effort as a means to mastery.

Curiosity as a Catalyst: Nurturing an Inquisitive Nature

Curiosity is the gasoline that sparks the flames of lifelong learning. In this section, we dig into the function of curiosity as a catalyst for inquiry, discovery, and intellectual engagement. Discover ways to cultivate and retain curiosity, ensuring that it becomes a driving force in your pursuit of knowledge.

Adaptability in a Changing World: The Lifelong Learner's Superpower

The 21st century is defined by fast change, and adaptability is a superpower possessed by lifelong learners. Explore the value of adaptation in navigating altering landscapes, accepting new technology, and prospering in dynamic contexts. Uncover practical ways for honing your flexibility and staying adaptable in the face of change.

Reflection and Self-Awareness: Keys to Continuous Improvement

Lifelong learners participate in a cycle of reflection and self-awareness that promotes ongoing progress. This part addresses the value of reflection in the learning process, including tools for measuring your success, identifying areas for growth, and setting meaningful goals. Discover how self-awareness becomes a compass guiding your lifelong learning path.

Building a Learning Network: The Power of Connection

A learning network is a web of relationships that amplifies the lifelong learning experience. We'll investigate how to develop and nurture a learning network, spanning mentors, peers, online groups, and thought leaders. Understand how varied perspectives and collaborative learning boost your comprehension and expand your horizons.

Time Management and Prioritization: Balancing Learning with Life

Effectively managing time is a vital skill for lifelong learners. We'll delve into time management tactics that find a balance between study goals and other living commitments. From prioritization tactics to building regular routines, learn how to integrate learning easily into your daily life.

Continuous Feedback: The Lifelong Learner's GPS

Feedback is a critical element in the lifelong learning path. We'll examine the value of seeking feedback from multiple sources, including mentors, peers, and self-assessment. Understand how continual feedback works as a GPS, providing guidance, correction, and insights that move you forward on your learning path.

Embracing Challenges and Uncomfortable Learning: The Path to Mastery

Lifelong learners aggressively seek difficulties and embrace discomfort as a way of growth. Explore the concept of unpleasant learning, when the quest of mastery includes venturing outside your comfort zone. Discover ways to conquer fears, increase resilience, and convert challenges into opportunities for profound learning.

Documenting Your Learning Journey: The Learning Journal

A learning notebook becomes a concrete record of your lifelong learning journey. We'll discuss the benefits of maintaining a learning journal, including prompts and examples to help you chronicle your experiences, thoughts, and milestones. Understand how reflection through writing promotes self-awareness and deepens the learning process.

Balancing Depth and Breadth: The T-Shaped Learner

The T-shaped learner combines significant competence in a given domain with a broad awareness of various subjects. Explore the concept of balancing depth and breadth in your learning activities, ensuring that you become a well-rounded individual with both specialized talents and a varied knowledge base.

Celebrating Milestones and Successes: Motivation for the Journey

Celebrating milestones and triumphs is a critical component of keeping motivation on the lifelong learning journey. We'll discuss the value of appreciating achievements, both big and small, and explore how celebrations serve as fuel for continuing learning and perseverance.

Resilience in the Face of Setbacks: The Lifelong Learner's Armor

Setbacks are inevitable, but resilience is the armor that protects the lifelong learner. Learn ways to foster resilience, bounce back from disappointments, and use setbacks as stepping stones toward greater success. Understand how a resilient mentality converts adversity into avenues for learning and growth.

Teaching as a Form of Learning: The Mentor-Learner Dynamic

The mentor-learner dynamic is a powerful part of lifelong learning. This section discusses the premise that teaching is a form of learning, as the act of transferring knowledge enhances comprehension. Discover the benefits of mentorship and explore how taking on the role of a mentor helps your learning path.

Integrating Lifelong Learning into Your Lifestyle: Sustainable Habits

Lifelong learning is not a separate undertaking but a way of life. We'll provide practical tips on incorporating lifelong learning into your lifestyle through sustainable practices. From microlearning to setting realistic goals, discover how to make learning an essential part of your everyday routine.

Legacy and Impact: Lifelong Learning Beyond the Individual

The value of lifelong learning extends beyond personal development. This section analyzes how lifelong learners contribute to societal growth, innovation, and the well-being of future generations. Understand the concept of leaving a legacy through knowledge-sharing, mentorship, and contributing to the communal pool of human learning.

As we close this chapter, you stand at the brink of a lifelong learning mindset a dynamic approach that transcends traditional concepts of schooling. Cultivating this mindset is not only about accumulating knowledge; it's a dedication to constant development, adaptation, and the quest for mastery. The trip is continuing, and the attitude you create will be your loyal companion, guiding you through the twists and turns of a lifetime filled with learning and progress. Get ready to embrace the lifelong learning attitude, and observe how it affects not just what you know but also who you become in the process. The adventure of a lifetime awaits a trip where learning knows no limitations, and the possibilities are as unlimited as your curiosity and determination allow.

Conclusion

A Prelude To Endless Discovery

As we shut the curtains on this investigation of the 21st-century learner, it's not an end but a beginning to the unlimited possibilities awaiting your voracious curiosity. The voyage of the 80-20 learner, the seeker of efficiency, the master of skills, and the lifelong enthusiast, is a continual quest a dance on the edge of what's known and the infinite expanses of what is yet to be discovered.

In the preceding chapters, we dug into the art and science of learning, revealing the secrets of efficient knowledge absorption, accelerating skill development, and smoothly incorporating technology into the learning tapestry. We navigated the landscapes of mnemonics, sharpened skills via purposeful practice, and harnessed the power of a growth mindset to turn hurdles into stepping stones toward mastery.

The digital era disclosed its jewels, from online platforms and educational apps to immersive technology and adaptive learning systems, giving you a vast palette to paint your learning canvas. We cultivated a lifelong learning mindset a dynamic approach that accepts difficulties, adapts to change, and thrives on a continuous drive for the better.

As you stand on the verge of the last chapter, consider this not an ending but a call to action. The 80-20 learner doesn't rest on laurels but rather sees each conclusion as a springboard to a new beginning. Your learning journey, now equipped with insights, techniques, and a mindset created for everlasting growth, is poised for boundless discovery.

Imagine the chapters yet to be written the talents yet to be learned, the knowledge yet to be discovered, and the ideas yet to be developed. The pages of your learning story are boundless, awaiting the indelible marks of your curiosity and determination. The conclusion of one chapter just signifies the turn of a page towards the next adventure.

So, reader, as you set down these pages, let them be not a closure but an invitation an invitation to continue the journey, to seek, to study, and to become the architect of your infinite intellectual odyssey. The 80-20 learner doesn't linger in conclusion; they march courageously into the unexplored frontiers of knowledge, equipped with the wisdom obtained and the yearning for what lies beyond.

May your path be ever vivid, your curiosity ever unquenchable, and your desire for learning a flame that never wanes. The story continues, the adventure persists, and endless possibilities await your exploration. Until the next chapter, where the quest for knowledge is not simply a choice but a way of life may your learning path be as endless as your curiosity allows.